Soltando Amarras

Casting Off

Poems by
Claribel Alegría

Translated by
Margaret Sayers Peden

Curbstone Press

FIRST EDITION, 2003
Copyright © 2003 by Claribel Alegría
Translation copyright ©2003 by Margaret Sayers Paden
ALL RIGHTS RESERVED.

Printed in Canada on acid-free paper by Transcontinental / Best Book

Cover design: Susan Shapiro
Cover art: "Nuestra Canción" by Alfredo Casteñeda, oil on canvas, signed
and dated 1999; courtesy of Mary-Anne Martin/Fine Art, New York.

This book was published with the support of
the Connecticut Commission on the Arts,
the National Endowment for the Arts,
AND donations from many individuals.
We are very grateful for all of this support.

Connecticut Commission
on the Arts

NATIONAL
ENDOWMENT
FOR THE ARTS

Library of Congress Cataloging-in-Publication Data

Alegría, Claribel.
    [Soltando Amarras. English & Spanish]
    Soltando Amarras = Casting off / poems by Claribel Alegría ;
translated by Margaret Sayers Peden.
        p. cm.
    ISBN 1-880684-98-5 (pbk.)
    I. Title: Casting off. II. Peden, Margaret Sayers. III. Title.

PQ7539.A47 S7613 2003
861'.64—dc21

                                    2002035165

published by
CURBSTONE PRESS   321 Jackson Street   Willimantic, CT 06226
        phone: 860-423-5110   e-mail: info@curbstone.org
                http://www.curbstone.org

A mis hijos,
    Maya, Patricia, Karen y Erik

For My Children,
    Maya, Patricia, Karen, and Erik

Vivo sin vivir en mí
    y de tal manera espero

       que muero porque no muero

           —Santa Teresa de Jesus

Contents

Soltando Amarras

Casting Off

Aracne

He tejido con mi vida
un laberinto
soy la araña en el centro
y es mi realidad
la que me hechiza.
Descubro caminos que ya anduve
y otros que están a medio andar
o se quedaron truncos.
Se me juntan todos
por la noche
en mis sueños se juntan
y una lenta polvareda
los enturbia.
Soy la araña en el centro
se me secó la baba
y me quedé sin hilo:
Una araña sin hilo
extraviada en su dédalo.

Arachne

I have woven with my life
a labyrinth
I am the spider at the center
and it is my reality
that bewitches me
I discover pathways already traveled
others cut short in mid-journey
or leading to dead ends.
They all come together
in the night
come together in my dreams
where they are obscured
in a gentle cloud of dust.
I am the spider at the center
My spittle dried up
and I ran out of thread.
A threadless spider
lost in its maze.

Lluvia

Mientras cae la lluvia
trastabillando entre las piedras
voy soltando recuerdos.
Es como si la lluvia
me punzara las sienes.
Chorrean
chorrean en desorden
los recuerdos:
la desgastada voz
de la sirvienta
contándome cuentos
de fantasmas.
Se sentaban a mi orilla
los fantasmas
y crujía la cama.
Aquella tarde lívida
en que supe que te irías para siempre.
El guijarro brillante
que de tanto palparlo
se convirtió en cometa.
Cae
cae la lluvia
y siguen fluyendo mis recuerdos
y me muestran un mundo
insensato
voraz
mundo-abismo
emboscada
torbellino
aguijón
y yo lo sigo amando
porque sí

Rain

As the falling rain
trickles among the stones
memories come bubbling out.
It's as if the rain
had pierced my temples.
Streaming
streaming chaotically
come memories:
the reedy voice
of the servant
telling me tales
of ghosts.
They sat beside me
the ghosts
and the bed creaked
that purple-dark afternoon
when I learned you were leaving forever,
a gleaming pebble
from constant rubbing
becomes a comet.
Rain is falling
falling
and memories keep flooding by
they show me a senseless
world
a voracious
world-abyss
ambush
whirlwind
spur
but I keep loving it
because I do

por mis cinco sentidos
por mi asombro
porque cada mañana
porque siempre lo he amado
sin entender por qué.

because of my five senses
because of my amazement
because every morning,
because forever, I have loved it
without knowing why.

Viaje hacia mí

Huyo hacia mí
hacia mi centro
me desnudo en el viaje
me libero
vuelvo a ser inocente.
He tomado distancia
de la vida
y me encaro a la muerte.

Voyage Toward Myself

I flee toward myself
toward my center
I throw off my clothes on the voyage
liberate myself
am innocent again.
I have put distance between myself
and life
and stand confronting death.

Mordedura

La tristeza es más triste
cuando nace del gozo
de aquel gozo esfumante
que compartí contigo
y me muerde a mí sola
cuando menos lo espero.

Bite

Sadness is all the sadder
when born of pleasure
of that fading pleasure
I shared with you
alone, it gnaws at me
when I least expect it.

Vuelta a Deyá sin ti

Estoy anclada en el presente
todo mi pasado en el presente
recupero mis gestos
abro como antes las persianas
no más crespones negros
me deslumbro ante el Teix
antes los rostros esculpidos
en el Teix
míos de nuevo
el azul del mar
desde las rocas
el ulular de los torrentes
los rebaños de ovejas
las miradas
las voces
y todo es igual
y se transforma todo.
Subo a pasos lentos
la escalera
saludo al árbol que sólo a mí
me pertenece
y sabe que soy otra
pero aún soy la misma.
La luz está cambiando
Se ha vuelto rosa el Teix
contemplo tu silla
en la terraza
y levanto mi copa.
Estás conmigo, amor
pero tampoco estás.

Return to Deyá Without You

For Bud

I am anchored in the present
all my past in the present
I do all the old things
I open the shutters as before
no more black mourning
I sit dazzled before the Teix
facing the sculpted faces
on the Teix
mine again
the blue of the sea
from the rocks
the yodeling of torrents
flocks of sheep
glances
voices
and everything is the same
and everything is transformed.
With halting steps I climb
the stairs
I greet the tree that belongs
to me alone
that knows I am a different woman
yet also the same.
The light is changing
the Teix is bathed in pink.
I stare at your chair
on the terrace
and lift a glass.
You are with me, my love
and yet you are not here.

Diste el salto mortal

Diste el salto mortal
y renaciste
yo sigo en esta orilla
agazapada

You Made the Great Leap

You made the great leap
and were reborn
I am left on this shore
crouched to spring

Huracán Mitch

En Posoltega
explotó el cementerio
y salieron los muertos
de sus tumbas
y lloraron
y fueron de nuevo
sepultados por el lodo
junto a los vivos que corrían
dando gritos
y elevando sus brazos
¿hacia quién?

Hurricane Mitch

In Posoltega
the cemetery exploded
and the dead came out
of their tombs
and wept
and were buried again
by the mud
along with the living who fled
screaming
and lifting their arms
to whom?

Dionisios

A Friedly

Me recuerdas a Cristo.
Tú,
coronado de hojas
El,
de espinas
dispensadores ambos
del amor
y el vino.

Dionysius

For Friedly

You remind me of Christ.
You,
crowned with leaves.
He,
with thorns
bestowers both
of love
and wine.

Tiresias

Tiresias es mi nombre
soy andrógino
y vivo entre dos mundos:
el que me dio aquel goce
de acariciar colores
con los cinco sentidos
y éste de mis sueños augurales.
Dos pájaros mis mundos
dos estrellas
que se evitan
se encuentran
se persiguen.
Camino a tropezones
sombra negra
y sombra iluminada.
Me rodean los pobres
los enfermos
los poetas
y me hablan de la tierra
y su dolor
y recuerdo la tierra
la mutilada tierra
el planeta quemado por los hombres
devastado
saqueado por los hombres
y los hombres destruyéndose
a sí mismos.
Sombra oscura
y sombra iluminada.
Ví a Venús bañándose desnuda
y la luz de sus aguas me cegó,
mas ella,

Tiresias

Tiresias is my name
I am androgynous
and I live between two worlds:
the one that gave me the pleasure
of caressing colors
with all five senses
and this world of prophetic dreams.
Two birds my worlds
two stars
that avoid each other
meet each other
pursue each other.
I stumble along
black shadow
and illuminated shadow.
I am surrounded by the poor
the sick
the poets
and they speak to me of the earth
and its pain
and I remember the earth
the mutilated earth
the planet scorched by men
devastated
and sacked by men
men destroying
themselves.
Dark shadow
and illuminated shadow.
I saw Venus bathing nude
and the light of her waters blinded me,
but she,

condolida,
me ungió de profecía
y soy un desterrado.
El mundo sangra
se desangra frente a mí
lo construyen los hombres
lo destruyen.
Más allá de la luna llegarán
caerán al infierno
a las tinieblas
no quiero ser profeta
oigo sollozar a los terrestres,
a mis dioses lejanos:
Apolo
Artemisa
Pan
que ya no son los mismos
de lo que antes fueron.
Sombra oscura
y sombra iluminada
dos pájaros mis mundos
dos estrellas.

sympathetic,
anointed me with prophecy
and now I am an exile.
The world is bleeding
bleeding to death before my eyes
men are constructing it
destroying it.
They will travel beyond the moon
they will fall into hell
into darkness
I do not want to be a prophet
I want to hear the earth-dwellers sob
to my distant gods:
Apollo
Artemisa
Pan
who are not the same
as before.
Dark shadow
and illuminated shadow
two birds my worlds
two stars.

Haikú

Día tras día
Se despierta cantando
El olmo viejo.

Haiku

Day after new day
the old elm tree awakens
spreads its limbs and sings.

Atropos

Atropos
hija de la noche
inflexible
inevitable
la más pequeña de las parcas
pero la más temible.
Atropos
la que rige destinos
y no se deja intimidar
ni con cantos
ni con rezos
ni con lloros.
Consagrada a la luna
lleva túnica blanca
y la vemos venir.
De todo nos despoja
no respeta niñez
juventud
señorío
su crueldad intoxica.
Las tijeras de Atropos
son de acero
y va segando vidas
como si fueran rosas.

Atropos

Atropos
daughter of night
inflexible
inevitable
the smallest of the Fates
but the most to be feared.
Atropos
she who rules destinies
and will not be intimidated
not with songs
not with prayers
not with weeping.
Consecrated to the moon
she wears a luminous tunic
and we can see her approaching.
She strips us of everything,
contemptuous of childhood
youth
old age,
her cruelty is dizzying.
The scissors of Atropos
are made of steel
and they click along snipping lives
as if they were roses.

Ahora

Ahora
en esta hora
crepita más la muerte
que la vida.

Now

Now
at this hour
death has more spark
than life.

New York-Madrid

No me gusta este vuelo
es un vuelo encerrado
sin libertad
sin alas
con una meta fija
y pasaporte.
Ansío el otro
el que yo sola emprenderé
no importa si está oscuro
y me sienta perdida.
Serán mías mis alas
fragmentos de mi vida
saltarán a mi encuentro
toda mi vida en haces
de luces
y de sombras
de nada me arrepiento
salvo de algunas cosas que no hice
amo tanto mi luz
como mi sombra
pero quizá me encuentre
ante un abismo
(vida y muerte
da igual)
y para siempre sepa
que el abismo soy yo
que todo cabe en mí
que soy mi propio dios.

New York-Madrid

For Luz and Mario

I don't like this flight
I'm too locked-in
no freedom
no wings
only a fixed destination
and a passport.
I long for that other flight
the one I will undertake alone
it won't matter if it's dark
and I feel lost.
My wings will be mine
fragments of my life
will leap to meet me
all my life in clusters
of lights
and shadows
I regret nothing
except some things I didn't do
I love my light as much
as my shadow
but maybe I will find myself
on the edge of an abyss
(life and death
no different)
and know for eternity
that the abyss is me
that all things fit within me
that I am my own god.

Destinos

Somos las furias
las erinias
las de siniestras alas
de murciélago.
Nacimos de la tierra
de tres gotas de sangre
que Urano derramó
sobre la tierra.
Son negros nuestros cuerpos
tenemos serpientes por cabellos
y cabezas de perro.
En nuestras manos brillan
azotes tachonados de metal.
Ingrato nuestro oficio
perseguidoras somos
vengadoras
con afán de justicia.
Enloquecimos a Orestes
le dimos muerte a Edipo
y lo lloramos.
Hicimos penitencia:
en el fuego sagrado
quemamos nuestras alas
que brotaron de nuevo
agigantadas.
Somos las más temidas
por temor nos adulan
nos llaman bondadosas
y en susurros pronuncian
nuestros nombres.
Cumplimos un destino
¿pero quién lo fraguó?

Destinies

We are the Furies
the Erinyes
they of the sinister
bat wings.
We are born of the earth
of three drops of blood
Uranus spilled
onto the earth.
Black are our bodies
serpents writhe
on our dog-like heads.
Metal-studded scourges
flash in our hands.
Our office is thankless
we are pursuers
avengers
we thirst for justice.
We drove Orestes mad
we killed Oedipus
and we weep for him.
We did our penance:
in the sacred fire
we burned our wings
which budded anew
made large.
We are feared above all others
adulated out of fear
called generous
our names spoken
in whispers.
We fulfilled a destiny
but who forged it?

un oscuro destino
que golpea
que impele
hacemos nuestra ronda
no hay perdón.
Somos las tres furias solitarias
las más viejas
en los confines del Olimpo.
¿Quién habló de piedad?
Sólo el destino existe
ese destino-abismo
que nos tumba
nos succiona
nos lanza
no nos deja escapar.

a dark destiny
that spurs
and incites us
we make our rounds
without forgiveness.
We are the three solitary Furies
the oldest
here on Olympus.
Who spoke of mercy?
Nothing exists but destiny
that destiny-abyss
that engulfs us
draws us in
thrusts us out
refuses us escape.

Aún

Aún sigo persiguiéndome
mordiéndome
buscándome
regresando a la infancia
a las raíces
pronosticando muertes
las mías
las posibles
ansiando ver mi rostro
el que encierra a los otros
el único
el final
y aunque aún no lo admita
temiéndole al encuentro.

Still

I am still chasing after myself
nipping at my heels
looking for myself
going back to my childhood
to my roots
predicting deaths
mine
possible deaths
yearning to see my face
the face that contains all others
the one
the final face
and though still not admitting it
fearing that encounter.

Vejez

Mientras mi futuro
empequeñece,
el pasado,
convertido en ahora
cuando evoco
me atrapa entre sus redes.

Old Age

As my future
grows shorter
the past
when summoned
converted into now
traps me in its nets.

Resurrección

A Benny

Perdí a la niña
que habitaba en mí
perdí a la adolescente
y a la joven
y a la mujer madura.
Inesperadamente
una luz en la sombra:
surgen hadas
sirenas
caballos de madera
paladines
dragones
se dilatan mis ojos
se me arrebola el rostro
todo dura un instante
pero he resucitado
con la risa de un niño
se revirtió mi tiempo.

Resurrection

For Benny

I lost the little girl
who lived in me
I lost the adolescent
and the young woman
and the mature woman.
Unexpectedly
a light in the shadow:
fairies emerge
sirens
wooden horses
paladins
dragons
my eyes open wide
my cheeks flush with color
everything lasts but an instant
I have revived
with the laugh of a child
time has reversed its course.

Te has convertido, Muerte

Te has convertido
Muerte
en el favorito de mis juegos
te invoco en la vigilia
me visitas en sueños
te invito
no te invito
me escondo
te sorprendo
te encuentro en el espejo
oscuramente
tejes una guirnalda
palpo mi calavera
y de pronto te escurres
con mi vida
y mi muerte
entre tus manos.

You Have Changed, Death

You have changed
Death
into the favorite of my games
I invoke you in my sleepless hours
you visit me in dreams
I invite you
I don't invite you
I hide
I surprise you
I find you in the mirror
darkly
you weave a garland
I touch my skull
and suddenly you scurry away
with my life
and my death
in your hands.

Cómo me duele el tacto

Cómo me duele el tacto
Cuando extiendo mi brazo
Y no te encuentro.

The Ache of Absence

Oh how my fingertips ache
when I hold out my hand
and don't find you.

Jano

Soy el más desdichado
entre los dioses
mis dos rostros hieráticos
contemplan el pasado
y el futuro.
El pasado me oprime.
Guerras
calaveras
y desastres
coronan el futuro.
El presente se escurre
sin que yo lo perciba.

Janus

I am the unhappiest
among the gods
my two hieratic faces
contemplate the past
and the future.
The past oppresses me.
Wars
skulls
disasters
crown the future.
The present slips away
without my perceiving it.

Máscaras

Soy todo lo que fui
lo que pude haber sido
lo que soñé y no fui
todos esos retazos incongruentes
que componen mi máscara
y me arañan el rostro
en mis noches de insomnio.
Soy todo lo que amo
los que me aman
y también mis fracasos
y mis lloros
y mis angeles mudos
y mis antepasados silenciosos.
Soy este oscuro tedio
que me opaca las horas
que me roe los huesos
que me atrapa
y me impide soltarme
y danzar hacia ti.

Masks

"All I was
all I was not
all that am I."
—F. Pessoa

I am all that I was
all I could have been
what I dreamed but was not
all the mismatched scraps
that compose my mask
and claw my face
through sleepless nights.
I am everything I love
all those who love me
and also my failures
my weeping
my mute angels
my silent ancestors.
I am this dark tedium
that clouds my hours
that gnaws my bones
that traps me
and prevents my breaking loose
to dance my way toward you.

Mi gata

A Sabrina

Cómo envidio a mi gata
que no sufre de insomnio
sobre el sofá se duerme
sobre el piso
si la despierta un ruido
abre apenas los ojos
y los vuelve a cerrar.
Me atrae su indolencia
su levedad
su holgura.
No se somete a nadie
su despertar es lento
hace yoga mi gata
viene hacia mí
se acerca
contra mi piel se frota
la acaricio
me araña
se escabulle de un salto.
¿Me quiere?
¿No me quiere?
Misteriosa es mi gata
y jamás lo sabré.

My Cat

for Sabrina

How I envy my cat
who never suffers from insomnia
she sleeps on the sofa
or on the floor
and if a noise wakes her
her eyes open, barely,
and then close again.
I am seduced by her idleness
her lightness
her poise
she bows to no one.
She wakes very slowly,
my cat, does her yoga,
starts toward me
closer, closer,
and rubs against me.
I stroke her
she scratches me
and skitters away with a leap.
She loves me?
she loves me not?
Mysterious is my cat.
and I shall never know.

Limbo

Me siento a gusto
en este limbo
acompañada sólo
de mis muertos.

Limbo

I feel good
in this limbo
all alone
with my dead.

Narciso

Qué lástima
Narciso
no llegó tu belleza
a culminar.
No arrugaron tu rostro
ni el dolor
ni el amor hacia otros
ni el claro oscuro de la espera.
Es vana tu mirada
persigue el reflejo
de tu imagen
y nada alrededor
y nada que surja
desde adentro.
Quizá no tengas dentro
quizá   te sientas huérfano
y eso te perfila
y te enajena:
eres tú el universo
y sólo tú existes
jamás un pensamiento
que te surque la frente
ni una lágrima oscura
que empañe tus pupilas.

Narcissus

What a pity
Narcissus
that your beauty
never matured.
Your face was never wrinkled
by sorrow
or by love for others
or by the chiaroscuro of hope.
Your gaze is vanity
it follows the reflection
of your image
but not anything around you
or anything rising
from within you.
Perhaps there is nothing within you
perhaps you feel orphaned
and that isolates you
alienates you:
you are the universe
and only you exist
never a thought
furrows your brow
never a dark tear
clouds your eyes.

Santa Ana

Aún no me desprendo
de Santa Ana
he vuelto muchas veces
no me quedo.
La camino
la abrazo
soy un tigre en acecho
rondando sus confines.
Cada vez que me adentro
empiezo a sollozar.

Santa Ana

I still cannot let go
of Santa Ana
I have come back many times
I don't stay.
I walk through it
I embrace it
I am a tiger on a trail
circling its limits.
Every time I walk deep into it
I begin to sob.

Ayer al mediodía

Ayer al mediodía
el silbido de un tren
que nunca apareció.
Seguí caminando por el campo
mientras rumiaba versos
que un día pasarán
haciendo menos ruido
que el silbido de un tren.

Yesterday at Noon

Yesterday at noon
the whistle of a train
that never appeared.
I kept walking through the field
as I mulled over poems
that one day will pass by
making less noise
than the whistle of a train.

Antígona

Sepultaré a mi hermano
aunque yo muera
ignorando las leyes
del desamor.
Se equivoca Creonte
jamás lo dejaré
como pasto de aves.
He ungido mis brazos
de cólera
y dureza
para encender la hoguera
que ha de borrar su cuerpo.
Se equivoca Creonte
no somos timoratas las mujeres
ni envenenamos la razón
ni esquivamos el riesgo.
Sepultaré a mi hermano
sin miedo
y con amor.

Antigone

I shall bury my brother
though it mean my death
and ignore the laws
of enmity.
Creonte is mistaken
I will never leave Polynices
as food for the birds.
I have anointed my arms
with anger
and strength
to light the pyre
that will consume his body.
Creonte is mistaken
we women are not faint-hearted
we do not poison reason
neither do we shy from risk.
I shall bury my brother
without fear
and with love.

Mi sombra

Empiezo apenas a vislumbrar
mi sombra
ese lado oscuro que me encubre
que se ríe de mí
que se divierte
señala mis caídas
mis carencias
y no siento vergüenza
y las asumo
y me siento más rica
más gozosa
cuando pasa la luz
por tu camelia
y se sonroja el cielo.

My Shadow

I see the first hint of
my shadow
the darkness that engulfs me
that laughs at me
that is entertained
as it points out my falls
my failings
but I feel no shame
I accept them
and feel the richer
more satisfied
when the light moves over
your camellia
and a blush fills the sky.

Medea

No brota el llanto
de mis ojos
son estallidos secos
los que pueblan mi noche.
Asesiné a mis hijos
lo que yo más amaba
¿o te amo más, Jasón?
Los hijos de Jasón
su alegría
su orgullo
fui el brazo vengador
enterré nuestros sueños
los sueños que danzaban
como brasas alegres
encendiéndome el rostro.
Me abandonó Jasón
y los maté por él
Jasón
Jasón
Jasón
grito su nombre
aúllo
llevo a mis hijos muertos
contra el pecho
los arrullo
les canto
nada me queda
nada
me quedan las serpientes
las serpientes aladas
que tiran de mi carro
llevándome al destierro

Medea

Those are not tears
streaming from my eyes
only the dry sobs
that haunt my night.
I murdered my own sons
they whom I most loved—
or do I love you more, Jason?
Jason's sons
his happiness
his pride
I was the avenging arm
I buried our dreams
dreams that danced
like joyful embers
shedding warmth upon my face.
Jason abandoned me
because of him, I killed them
Jason
Jason
Jason
I shout your name
I howl
I clutch my dead sons
to my bosom
I rock them
I sing to them
I have nothing left
nothing
only the serpents are left
the winged serpents
that pull the chariot
carrying me to my exile

es más cruel el destierro
que la muerte
asesiné a mis hijos
veo sus sombras
creciendo hasta mis ojos
los cuerpos de mis hijos
sus luminosos cuerpos
desafiando el olvido.
Me quedé sin sus voces
sin sus juegos
sin sus mimos
para siempre seré la plañidera
andando
y desandando
en el desierto.
Es de muerte mi canto
y es de triunfo
lo hice por ti
Jasón
lo hice por tu amor
por tu amor que me diste
transformándome en diosa
y de súbito un día
me arrancaste.

exile more cruel
than death.
I murdered my sons
I see their shadows
growing before my eyes
my sons' bodies
their luminous bodies
defying oblivion.
I am left without their voices
without their games
without their loving play
I shall moan and weep forever
walking
and wandering
in the desert
my song is of death
and of triumph
I did it for you
Jason
I did it for your love
the love you gave me
transforming me into a goddess
until suddenly one day
you tore me out by the roots.

¿Dónde?

¿Dónde quedó el hechizo
de aquel río?
¿Dónde la voz del viento
silbándome al oído
la palabra precisa?
¿Qué fue de aquel asombro
ante cada amanecer
y cada ocaso?
¿Mi temor a la luna
mis plegarias?
Sin que me diera cuenta
se fue esfumando todo
me avergoncé de mi candor
y lo expulsé de mí.
Me he quedado sin cábalas
sin ritos
sin hechizos
mi rostro no es el mismo
día a día me miro en el espejo
 y me devuelve siempre
una imagen incierta.
Nada es eterno
nada
pero mi amor
perdura.

Where?

Where did it go
the spell of that river?
Where, the voice of the wind
whistling the precise word
into my ear?
What became of the amazement
that greeted each dawn
and each sunset?
My fear of the moon?
My prayers?
All of it faded
without my noticing
I was ashamed of my candor
and I purged myself of it.
I am left with no cabalas
no rites
no witchcraft
my face is not the same
every day I look in the mirror
and all it gives back
is a nebulous image.
Nothing is eternal
nothing
but my love
endures.

Camino a Damasco

Pensé que ahora sí
que estaba en mi camino
hacia Damasco
y vería una luz
que me tumbara
y sabría qué hacer
al levantarme.
He perdido la ruta
no hay señales
camino
camino hacia el final
cada vez más de prisa
hacia mi realidad inexorable
y todo es más oscuro
y no tengo respuestas
y me cansé ya
de preguntar.

Road to Damascus

I thought that finally
I was on my road
to Damascus
and that I would see a light
and fall to my knees
and know what to do
when I got up.
But I have lost my way
there are no signposts
I walk
I walk toward the road's ending
faster and faster
toward my inescapable reality
and everything grows darker
and I have no answers
and now I have grown weary
of asking.

Clamor de Francesca

"No hay mayor dolor que acordarse
del tiempo feliz en la miseria."
—Dante, El Inferno, Canto V

Nos atrapó el amor
quebrantamos las reglas
y un aire macilento
nos arrastró al infierno.
A través de borrascas
torbellinos
tormentas
el viento nos conduce
nos castiga
no hay tregua.
Viajo pegada a él
a mi Paolo
encadenada estoy a su costado
somos la misma sombra
el mismo grito somos
nuestros cuerpos se azotan
uno al otro
sin poder separarse.
No es el amor culpable
no tiene reglas el amor
alguien que nunca amó
imaginó este juego
y nos lanzó impasible
a la agonía eterna.

Francesca's Lament

> "There is no greater sorrow than to remember
> happy times in misery."
> —Dante, The Inferno, Canto V

We were entrapped by love,
we broke the rules
and were dragged down to hell
upon a light wind.
Through black clouds
whirlwinds
storms
the wind bears us
punishes us
allows no truce.
I travel close beside him
my Paolo
I am chained to his side
we are one shadow
one cry
we are whipped
against one another
bound, unable to part.
Love is not to blame
love has no rules
someone who never loved
imagined this game
and callously flung us
into eternal agony.

Salí de mí

Salí de mí
dejando atrás
el hoy y el mañana.
A mi regreso
eran huecas las voces
y nada comprendía.
Se me extravió el hilo
del coloquio
y no lo encuentro aún.

Outside Myself

I stepped outside myself
leaving behind
today and tomorrow.
When I returned
voices sounded hollow
and I understood nothing.
I lost the thread
of the conversation
and I haven't found it yet.

Difícil peso

Debo abrir mis compuertas
aligerar el peso
del amor
que escapen mis recuerdos
mis lágrimas
mis sueños
mis paisajes
mis muertos
que se los lleve el mar
más allá de mi barca
que floten ellos solos
y que me dejen sola.

Onerous Weight

I must open the floodgates
lighten the weight
of love
let my memories spill out
my tears
my dreams
my landscapes
my dead
let the sea carry them
far away from my ship
let them float off on their own
and leave me my solitude.

Retorno

El reposo no existe
movimiento hacia fuera
movimiento hacia dentro
caer
volar
caer
hacerse añicos
recoger los añicos
encontrar a ese ojo
que nunca parpadea
a la pupila insomne
que nos alcanza a todos
y de nuevo a la rueda
a la tierra en el rostro
a las alas de cera.

Return

There is no rest
thrust out
pull in
fall
fly
fall
shatter to bits
pick up the pieces
reach that eye
that never blinks
the sleepless pupil
that finds us everyone
and back again to the wheel
to dirt in the face
to the wings of wax.

Un horizonte nuevo

Un horizonte nuevo
se despliega ante mí
un horizonte que se abre
y me invita a entrar
para encontrarme
para ser devorada
liberada
y yo no tengo miedo
y danzo
y salto
y salgo de mi cuerpo
y vuelvo a entrar
y me siento incómoda
en mi cárcel
y quiero ser lanzada
dentro de esa frontera
que me incita
y me acerco
y me alejo
pero no he de tardar.

A New Horizon

A new horizon
is unfolding before me
a horizon that opens
and invites me to come in
to find myself
to be devoured
liberated
and I am not afraid
and I dance
and leap
and leave my body
and go back in again
and I feel restless
in my prison
and want to be launched
past that frontier
that so attracts me
and I approach
and I retreat
but I must hurry.

El Minotauro

"Soy hijo de la noche"
susurraste
para mí el laberinto
donde nutro mi cólera
y me arrincona la torpeza.
No bebí de los pechos
de mi madre
me acunó el desamor
me enamoré una vez de una doncella
y ella huyó de mí
y yo la perseguí
y la maté en mi abrazo.
Después de que así hablaste
fue mío tu misterio
había que inmolarte
eras distinto
el fuego de tus fauces
atravesó mi niebla
palpé tu desamparo
tu inocencia
tu exilio
te miré
me miraste
y nos cubrió el silencio.

The Minotaur

"I am the child of night,"
you whispered,
"mine the labyrinth
where I nurture my anger
and am trapped by languor.
I never nursed
at my mother's breasts
indifference molded me
once I loved a maiden
and she fled from me
and I pursued her
and killed her with my embrace."
After you spoke as you did
your mystery was mine
I had to immolate you
you were different
the fire from your gorge
blazed through my mist
I caressed your helplessness
your innocence
your exile
I looked at you
you looked at me
and silence closed about us.

Revelación

Caminé hacia el frutero
Y de pronto la uva
se convirtió en palabra.

Revelation

I walked toward the fruit bowl
and suddenly the grape
became word.

Casandra

Vete, Casandra,
vete.
Ha perdido la muerte
su inocencia
y nos muestra su máquina
infernal
pero el mundo no acaba.
Se transforma, Casandra,
se transforma.
Es doloroso el parto
dura siglos
milenios
y una raza nueva
gobernará la tierra
y cesarán las guerras
la violencia
los odios
se ensancharán los ríos
y crecerán los mares
y los bosques.
Es más prieta la noche
cuando la luz se acerca.
No se termina el mundo
se transfroma,
Casandra,
se transforma.

Cassandra

Go, Cassandra,
begone.
Death has lost
her innocence
and is showing us her infernal
machinery
but the world isn't ending,
it's changing, Cassandra,
it's changing.
The birth is agonizing
lasting centuries
millennia
and a new race
shall rule the earth
and wars
and violence
and hatred shall cease
the rivers will run wide
and the seas
and forests enrich the earth.
Night is darkest
before the light of dawn.
The world isn't ending,
it's changing,
Cassandra,
it's changing.

Soltando amarras

A pesar
de mi largo coloquio
con la muerte
me resulta difícil
desprenderme de mí
engendrarme a mí misma
concebirme.

Casting Off

Despite
my long conversation
with death
it is hard for me
to let go of myself
to engender myself
to conceive myself.

Desperté al día

Desperté al día
con tu imagen clavada
entre mis ojos
pensando en tu partida
en tus encuentros
en tus remotas playas
en tu amor que regresa
reverdece
me corona de estrellas.
Estoy al final
de mi circuito
hay rendijas abiertas
hay señales
puedo escuchar tu voz
escuchar los latidos
de tu voz
sin que importen apenas
las palabras.
¿Por qué obstinarme tanto
si empiezo a vislumbrar
tu cercanía?

I Awoke to the Day

I awoke to this day
with your image burned
into my eyes
thinking of your leaving
your encounters
your distant shores
your love that returns
buds anew
crowns me with stars.
I am reaching the end
of my cycle
there are widening fissures
there are signs
I can hear your voice
hear the throb
of your voice
how little the words
matter.
Why am I so obsessed
when I am beginning to glimpse
your nearness?

Divagaciones

Por fin he comprendido
que todo es pasajero
lanzo a volar mis yoes
y aguardo
vigilante
el porvenir
sin misterio la vida
sería irrespirable.

Digressions

Finally I have realized
that all things are fleeting
I fling away my many selves
and vigilant
I await
the future
without mystery life
would be suffocating.

Es hora ya de que te rindas

Es hora ya
de que te rindas
mi fatigoso
y fatigado cuerpo
dame el derecho de escapar.
En un tiempo te amé
eras fresco
gracioso
eras travieso.
Siento pena por ti
al caminar te encorvas
con cada movimiento hay un crujido
estás rígido
enjuto
y con barriga
pero pese a tus males
y a tus sordos gemidos
sigues queriendo ser.
Ese amor por la vida
que te abrasa
no te deja
dejarme.

It's Time Now to Give Up

It's time now
to give up,
my exhausting,
and exhausted body,
give me the right to escape.
There was a time I loved you
you were fresh
entertaining
mischievous.
I feel sorry for you
you are bent and stooped
and you creak with every step
you're stiff
gaunt
and you've grown a belly
but despite your ills
and your quiet moans
you still want to live.
That love for life
that inflames you
does not let you
leave me.

Lázaro

"La pena de los dioses es no
alcanzar la muerte"
                —Rubén Darío

Señor,
Señor,
¿por qué me has resucitado?
Lastima el sol mis ojos
no soy Lázaro ahora
no soy aquel que fui
ocupé mi sitio en las tinieblas
fui su huésped
me acarició la sombra.
Río de muerte soy,
ángel nocturno
fantasma de mí mismo
sarcófago ambulante.
No me quiten las vendas
no quiero ver las muecas de los míos
ni escuchar sus plañidos.
Entiérrenme de nuevo
¿por qué resucitar
a un mundo fugaz?
He visto el rostro de la muerte
he alcanzado la muerte
soy eterno.

Lazarus

"The gods' punishment is never
to know death"
—Rubén Darío

Lord,
Lord,
why have you revived me?
The sun hurts my eyes
I am not Lazarus now
I am not the one I was
I had my place in the darkness
I was its guest
shadow caressed me.
I am a river of death
angel of night
ghost of myself
walking sarcophagus.
Do not remove my graveclothes
I do not want to see the pain of my loved ones
or hear their plaints.
Bury me again
why be reborn to a fading world?
I have seen the face of death
I have achieved death
I am eternal.

Lilith

Te liberaste Lilith
dejaste el Paraíso
para crear tu estirpe
nunca quisiste ser
la mujer sometida
del aburrido Adán
desafiaste al vacío
inventaste la risa
estabas sola
sola
buscando infatigable
tu destino
del fondo de tu angustia
se levantó tu risa
bailaste ante la luna
una impúdica danza
y reíste
reíste
rayaste con tu risa
el universo.
Se sonrojó la luna
y te acunó en su seno
supiste en ese instante
que eras ángel caído
y por primera vez
sentiste a Dios
en ti.

Lilith

You freed yourself, Lilith,
you left Paradise
in order to found your line
you never wanted to be
the subservient wife of
that boring Adam
you defied the void
you invented laughter
you were alone
alone
tirelessly seeking
your fate
from the depths of your anguish
rose your laughter
you danced beneath the moon
a dance without shame
and you laughed
laughed
you raked the universe
with your laughter.
The moon blushed
and cradled you in her bosom
you knew at that instant
that you were a fallen angel
and for the first time
you felt God
within you.

Debo soltarte

A ti también
debo soltarte
descargarte del peso
de mi duelo
dejarte al fin a solas
con tu arcano.

I Must Let You Go

You, too,
I must let go
I must relieve you of the weight
of my mourning
leave you, finally, alone
with your enigma.

Fin de acto

Hacia la muda soledad
encamino mis pasos
hacia el silencio-estrella
que dejó ya de preguntar.

Curtain

My footsteps are leading
toward quiet solitude
toward the star-silence
that has no more questions.

Claribel Alegría was born in Estelí, Nicaragua in 1924, and grew up in El Salvador. She has long been recognized not only as a major poet but also as a major voice in the struggle for liberation in El Salvador and in Central America. She has published over forty books including poetry, novels and a book of children's stories. Many of her books have been translated into English, including editions from Curbstone Press of *Ashes of Izalco, Luisa in Realityland, Family Album, Fugues, Thresholds,* and *Sorrow.* She has received numerous awards for her poetry, including the Casa de las Américas Prize. Her recognition in the U.S. widened considerably when Bill Moyers interviewed her for his *Language of Life* series that first aired on PBS in 1995. Claribel Alegría and her husband Darwin J. Flakoll collaborated on a novel and a number of testimonies until his death in 1995. Vividly documenting key dramatic events in Latin American history, these testimonies as well as her poetry have earned her international recognition. Her poetry collection *Sorrow,* a lyric tribute to her departed husband and their life together in a moving exploration of grief, won the Independent Publisher Book Award (IPPY) for Poetry in 2000 and was honored by U.S. independent booksellers as a BookSense choice. Claribel Alegría currently resides in Managua.

In a long and distinguished career, **Margaret Sayers Peden** has translated thirty-seven books by such major Latin American authors as Isabel Allende, Laura Esquivel, Carlos Fuentes, Mario Vargas Llosa, Pablo Neruda, and Octavio Paz. Professor Emeritus of Spanish at the University of Missouri, she has received numerous awards and honors, including the Gregory Kolovakas Award from PEN and fellowships from the National Endowment for the Arts and the National Endowment for the Humanities. In 1998, she received a special homage by the Guadalajara International Book Fair, the American Literary Translators Association, and the University of Guadalajara for distinguished service to the arts. In 2001, she was elected an Honorary Member of the Hispanic Society of America.

CURBSTONE PRESS, INC.

is a non-profit publishing house dedicated to literature that reflects a commitment to social change, with an emphasis on contemporary writing from Latino, Latin American and Vietnamese cultures. Curbstone presents writers who give voice to the unheard in a language that goes beyond denunciation to celebrate, honor and teach. Curbstone builds bridges between its writers and the public – from inner-city to rural areas, colleges to community centers, children to adults. Curbstone seeks out the highest aesthetic expression of the dedication to human rights and intercultural understanding: poetry, testimonies, novels, stories, and children's books.

This mission requires more than just producing books. It requires ensuring that as many people as possible learn about these books and read them. To achieve this, a large portion of Curbstone's schedule is dedicated to arranging tours and programs for its authors, working with public school and university teachers to enrich curricula, reaching out to underserved audiences by donating books and conducting readings and community programs, and promoting discussion in the media. It is only through these combined efforts that literature can truly make a difference.

Curbstone Press, like all non-profit presses, depends on the support of individuals, foundations, and government agencies to bring you, the reader, works of literary merit and social significance which might not find a place in profit-driven publishing channels, and to bring the authors and their books into communities across the country. Our sincere thanks to the many individuals, foundations, and government agencies who support this endeavor: J. Walton Bissell Foundation, Connecticut Commission on the Arts, Connecticut Humanities Council, Daphne Seybolt Culpeper Foundation, Fisher Foundation, Greater Hartford Arts Council, Hartford Courant Foundation, J. M. Kaplan Fund, Eric Mathieu King Fund, John D. and Catherine T. MacArthur Foundation, National Endowment for the Arts, Open Society Institute, Puffin Foundation, and the Woodrow Wilson National Fellowship Foundation.

Please help to support Curbstone's efforts to present the diverse voices and views that make our culture richer. Tax-deductible donations can be made by check or credit card to:
Curbstone Press, 321 Jackson Street, Willimantic, CT 06226
phone: (860) 423-5110 fax: (860) 423-9242
www.curbstone.org

IF YOU WOULD LIKE TO BE A MAJOR SPONSOR OF A
CURBSTONE BOOK, PLEASE CONTACT US.